Infinite In My Heart

MARTINA E. FAULKNER

Copyright © 2018 Martina E. Faulkner
All rights reserved.
ISBN-13: 978-0-9963668-4-7
Library of Congress Control Number: 2018905118

DEDICATION

For everyone who has ever loved, lost love,
and still lives with the hope of new love.

CONTENTS

How…?	1
The Hardest Easy Thing	2
If I	5
Two From One: Pieces in a Tunnel	6
Falling	9
Could I	10
Nighttime	11
Ode to a Stranger	13
Tick-Tock-Tick	14
Can I Keep You?	15
5 Minutes	16
Held	18
Peppered by Hope	19
The In-between of Here and Nowhere	20
Eggplant Parmesan Upside-Down	22
Tethered	23
An Awakening	24
And Yet To…	25
Tears of Love	26
Love and Loss	27
Gifted	28
Paddling	29
Hidden In Sight	31
Angst.	32
Erosion	33
Navigation	34
The Mirror	35
…Farther Still	36
Think of Me	37
Churning, Turning, Swirling	38
What is Love?	40
Give Way!	41
Unified Duality	42
Branded Speechless	44
Through the Cracks…Love	45
About the Author	49

How…?

How is it possible
To love
More than I do
Myself
You

How is it possible
To feel
In my skin
Joy
Sin

How would it be
Feeling
Holding
Everything
In me

Breath, breathe in
Hold it
Closer now,
Yet farther
Still

15 January 2012

The Hardest Easy Thing

The scent of you is missing from me
My pillows
My hair
My scarf
No longer have you in them.

Your voice gone for too long
No whispers
No laughter
No teasing
Or funny voices have been heard

Under a dotted sky to say
I love you.

I love you
I can't choose you.

It's not perfect even though it was
Perfect, even though I know it's not.
It's exactly what we needed
At a time when we both needed
Something different
Something real
Something raw
Something easy.

Only it wasn't easy
It was effortless.

And still took too much
Out of me.

One of the hardest easy things was
Loving you.

And it can only be that way.
You are missing from me.
I feel myself missing from you,
And can't reach out.
I can't reach for you.

I've only ever wanted someone to reach for
For me
Until we aged away from youth
In our bodies
Not our hearts
Or souls.

We were meant for each other
For a time
For now
Not for always

But forever.

I will carry you
Where I go
Because it was perfect in its place.
We were perfect
For a while
Anyway.

I wish I had your scent again, I wish
My scarf
My pillows

My hair
Could remember
You.

It is only my heart that remembers.
Remembers the feel of

Your fingers on my arm
Your chest beneath my cheek
Your hand on my thigh.
My heart remembers.

It remembers.
It knows.
And my soul nods.

We were for each other.
Made
United
Broken
Until another day or time
When our souls glimpse perfection again
And smile.

If I

So many times
smiles became frowns.
So many times
I've been let down.

All I'm asking for now
is a little honesty.
All I need now
is faith and beauty.

If I gave you my heart
would you hold it dear?
If I gave you my heart
would you keep it near?

To love again
with an open heart
And trust that it's right
from the very start…

I'm asking you
to share in time
Your heart with me
in exchange for mine.

When I give away my heart
I will hold it dear.
When I give away my heart
I will always keep it near.

8 December 2010

Two from One: Pieces in a Tunnel

Strewn about the room
Chambers in my mind
Overflowing with the
Scattered pieces I find

Will it ever make sense, be easier?
Will I find the missing part
To piece together these
Shards of my heart?

Feel like stepping away
Leaving it all behind
Taking my name
Moving to a different place and time

Holding on here
Seems so far from what I know
Yet knowing I need to leave
Isn't easy all alone

Cleaning up the past
And making sense of it all
Like wandering through the ruins
While learning how to crawl

What is this surrounding
How did I get to where I am?
Was it love or something more
That made me take a stand?

Where can I catch the train
To where I want to go
So I don't live this life again
Because now I know

That giving my life to someone else
Is easier than it seems
But all too often it happens
At the expense of your own dreams

I've learned my lesson now
I'm ready to begin
But life still has me waiting
Though the tunnel's getting thin

In time the light will break through
And sunshine will be a while
But whilst I'm stuck inside I dream
Of the things that make me smile

It's the hope in what will be
The dream that's coming out
That keeps me moving slowly
And clears my soul of doubt

The future is more than bright
I've seen it at a glance
But tonight I draw the line
Tonight I make my stance

Don't you know how you've hurt me?
Don't you see what you've done?
Everything has ended
Now it's empty and time to run

The jagged edges linger when
Leaving the past behind
Still clinging to old stories whilst
Clearing out my mind

I will live for each new day
Brighter than before

Because I know deep in my heart
It's me I've waited for.

10 December 2010

Falling

Falling like snow
gentle
soft
full of promise and hope

that's how I want it to be
with big fluffy flakes
that rest on my nose

reminding me of the joy of
playing
laughing
like a child again

with a full heart
a belly of giggles
and a hint of awe
watching a shooting star

falling
like the first snow
that's how I wish it to be
when I fall in love again.

8 December 2010

Could I

Could I die loving you?
Not having been with you?
Would anything change,
would it be different
had we never met?

Would the love be the same?
Does it matter?
What is love anyway,
who is to say
how we love and live?

I could die today loving you
knowing that I had
felt joy that permeated my soul
and gratitude that changed
it all.

Yes - I could die loving you
And it would be enough.

Could I
Could you
Could we

Would I
Would you

Should we. . .

21 November 2010

Nighttime

Darkness holds me in its grip
Loneliness scents the air like cheap perfume
Always lingering, reminding, pestering
An itchy nose with no sneeze
Unfulfilling.

Nights symbolic of
Cozy blankets
Movies
Food

Are now empty and filled.

Mind-draining entertainment
Anything to avoid
Feeling
The reality
The phone.

The breaking point is always just out of reach
Triggered by a word
Or a picture
Or a lyric
Sometimes simply a chord.

Echoing notes of evenings past
Singing haunting melodies of
Lost dreams
Sacrifice

And Love.

It was always love
Even when it wasn't.

And the nighttime knows,
While the darkness keeps hold
Of the truth.

9 November 2010

Ode to A Stranger

If I needed a shoulder to cry on,
Could I have yours?

When I need someone to rely on,
Will you hold open those doors?

When strong arms are all that can hold me,
Will you outstretch your own?

And when I'm tired and lonely,
Will you welcome me home?

1 October 2010

Tick-Tock-Tick

There is a sadness
Without tears
That grips the heart
And won't let go

A leaden weight in the soul
Resting on every breath
And taking hold
Of time

The feathery antidote
Never relinquishing its gift
Completely
But in droplets

Time
Time
Time

Waiting heals and wounds
Waiting wounds and heals
Waiting heals wounds

Time
Time
Time

The clock is an ally
Friend and foe
Ticking away at life
Yet bringing hope

Inhale
Exhale
Breathe.
19 September 2010

Can I Keep You?

Can I keep you?
Just for me
Just for the moment

Hold you safe
Keep us hidden
Conceal our hearts

So the world doesn't muddy
The crystal waters
Or darken
The starlit skies

Keep you with me
Here
Now
Always.

2013

5 minutes

23:18
How is this 40?
Looking around at loss, and
Still grateful

Next to my head,
Only emptiness.

Headphones don't drown out
The chronic silence
A pervasive noise of emptiness
Of failure
Of choice.

Gotye hits a grand slam
In an empty stadium
Who could hear
Who listens
Even if the tree fell in attendance
Silence.

I used to know
I knew
I never knew
I never know
Which is better
Or best.

And the pillows are still fluffed
Dent-less, empty
The universe hates a void

But not tonight
It won't be filled.

You didn't have to
And you did
And the whirling dervishes
Won't let me sleep.
23:23

9 September 2012

Held

My heart
Found yours
A mirror
Love

My body
Found yours
A cushion
Home

My soul
Found yours
A sail
Freedom

You found me
In me
Where
I found you

My hand
Found yours
And
Held.

circa 2015

Peppered by Hope

Alone at night
With the green haze of numbers
Illuminating salty drops
Blurring their edges, resting in the fringes of sight.

Why?

It hurts.

My heart heavier
Than wet sand,
Still beating.
Breath lingers,
Heaving and thickened by tears.

Again.

Why?

Does understanding bring patience?
Does patience bring understanding?

I own neither.
Claim a life
Of confusion
Peppered by hope
Love
Loss
And breath.

30 May 2011

The In-between of Here and Nowhere

Trapped, I roam free
Searching, hoping - scared.

Fear is a cement shoe
With albatross wings
Gliding with the weight
Of a thousand worlds
Soaring in and out,
Running from shadows.

Do you hear me?

I can't hear myself
Tapping, knocking - endless.

Serenity in electronic heroin
Is a fleeting survival
The silence draws nearer
As a steady drum beats
In my ear, my neck, my mind

Salted ocean water-like droplets
Fall across a rosy-hued surface

Do you hear me?
In my silence.

In the in-between of here
And nowhere all at once
Meaningless has meaning
And up is always down

Guides ride horses and
Light breaks through the dawn

Resilience and reservation, yet
In freedom, I feel trapped.

Listen.

2 March 2010

Eggplant Parmesan Upside-Down

Because up is down and
Black is white.
Because square is round and
Day is night.

Sitting in blades of grass
Blades of sound
Would they slice me open
If I rolled around?

"I don't want you to replace
my eggplant parmesan,
I want to replace you!"

There, I said it out loud,
Inasmuch as subconscious streaming
Is speaking words or sentences
In thoughts with hidden meaning!

Now what?

Thoughts.

It's not that I want to end my life.
It's that I want my life as it exists to end.

31 October 2009

Tethered

Let me soar,
And be there when I cry.
Hold me close
And let me fly.

With face in the sun
A rooster floats by in a swirl.
My palms caress rock faces
Feeling the immensity twirl.

I walk the earth,
I walk the stars,
Ageless and timeless
I'm uncovering my scars.

I am more myself
When you hold my space.
Giving me freedom
In the midst of your embrace.

An Awakening

Like an alarm in my heart,
You've awakened me.

Aroused all that is real,
Joyful
Promised
In this life.

Stirring words gave breath to my soul
Your presence jarring my mind.

Life vibrates all around me, in
Color
Song
And your touch

Strumming, your guitar hums
Yet I am so far away,

I hear you in my heart
Until my hand
Finally rests
In yours.

14 March and 20 May 2013

And Yet To…

And all I can hear
Is a voice in my ear
Whispering and shouting your name.

To know your soul
Is too far to hold
My heart echoes in silent refrain.

Still the silence grows
As the four winds blow
A dark moon rising above.

Inviting me once more

To rest by your side
In the fires of pride
Asleep in the night of love.

18 April 2013

Tears of Love

When I die lights go out
Flowers weep petals of tears

When I die, will you cry?
Will tears stream down
And burn your eyes?
Will you weep for me
From across the sea?

Or

Will you sing me a song
From so high above
Melodies of joy
For the miracle of love?

Will you hold my memory dear
Singing out loud for all to hear?
Or quietly hum my tune
Alone in your room?

11 May 2013

Love and Loss

I lost everything to gain
The only thing: myself.
All that is lost is minor,
And at moments, gargantuan.

Like a severed limb glimpsed resting on the ground,
Knowing there is no way to reattach it,
Knowing that it is already dead,
Yet longingly gazing for what it once was or could have been.

The mind is not my friend in moments like these.
It chatters with the cacophony of a thousand birds at sunset.
The noise is deafening inside me.
It drowns out any melody continuously playing in my soul.
The melody of angels,
Divine music by which I set my compass,
To heal the anguish of my soul.

At moments like these, survival kicks in,
Hopefully,
And fear takes its stranglehold,
Woefully.

I know.

A light-shining heart will always recognize another,
Thankfully.

26 May 2013

Gifted

I was quite spoiled today.
Loved.
By three magical songs
in the morning,
A thoughtful melodic gift via the post
in the afternoon,
And a bouquet of digital flowers
sent one by one.

Unconventional,
conventional,
thoughtful and loving.

I go to sleep happy, loved
and contentedly peaceful.
Feeling safer.
Grateful.

19 June 2013

Paddling

Lost.
Adrift.

Nowhere to go.
Do you trust the current?
Or the tide?

Will it carry me? Away or toward
Who I am.
And you?

Not floating easily
Bobbing up and down
Choppy
And
Scared.

Dangling in the vastness
Of spilt ink,
Feeling weightless
With full shoulders
Laden
Bare.

It could be,
But it's not.
Because it takes more time
And nerve
Stress
To get there.

And I feel so alone
Just bobbing
Floating
Sailing

Not knowing
And still paddling.

It's in the paddles that the mystery loses the game.
It's in the paddles where the sense is lost.
It's in the paddles where falsehood lies.
Dropping paddles in ink.
God give me strength.

9 July 2013

Hidden In Sight

Nobody sees her cry
Or the tears that fall
Behind dry eyes.

11 July 2013

Angst.

Awake.
Alone.
Attacked like a rogue wave from behind
Consuming.
Enveloping.

No room to breathe,
While spindly tips of frayed endings
Shoot fire like summer lightning.

Waiting.
Giving in.
Holding off.
Which way to go?

Pins and needles saturate my trillions.
Leaded lungs barely lift enough to expand
Yet contract repeatedly in quick succession.

Let it pass.
It will pass.
A small white circle helps
Sometimes.

25 July 2013

Erosion

Trust, like sand
Glides through my fingers
Cascading in piles at my feet
Never to be a castle

Each passing hour
Burns down into
Fading embers of
An extinguished flame

How close we were
How far away
How bright our dawn
How dark the day
How much we knew
How little we thought
How long this was, yet
How fast
It all fell
Apart.

Navigation

The mast to my sail
Strong and Steadfast
Holding me to flutter
And catch the wind

Carrying us to foreign lands
Stretching over every horizon
Breezes fuel our love
With sunshine our guidepost

21 October 2013

The Mirror

Joy is contagious
Like breath is necessary
Encompassing me – joy consumes
And expands all that I touch

Without love there is no joy
Joy lives in my presence
Like breath in my lungs
Pounding my heart

Hot coals under my feet
Burn and empower the trust
That is found in
Faith

Nothing holds nature's container
But trust – emboldened by
The consistent paw prints that silently
Surround me as music plays

Terrified of the dark water
I am blind, rudderless
Blackness shines through
To my heart on uncharted maps
Leading me on, as I gaze upon
My reflection.

11 April 2013

...Farther Still

It was a moment
A touch
Not forever
But enough.

For just one day
We escaped it all,
No reality invading us
The world seemed to stall.

We met again
And strolled for hours
Amidst the hills
Among your flowers.

There is no weird silence
We know too well who we are

It's as if we were destined
By some guiding star.

We had our day
And then it was two.
Living together in a moment
Before returning to truth.

It wasn't enough.
I doubt it could ever be,
Unless we meet again one day
When we are both free.

When I am for you
And you are for me.

2017

Think of Me

When the birdsong floats through morning dew
And wild morning glories greet you with each step
With hedgehogs scurrying from their slumber

I am all around you
In everything you see
In all you hear
Feel
Smell

The rose's perfume carries my song to you
My smile echoed in the evening call
Each bark-covered limb the sound of my touch

As the sun waxes into fullness
Like the gentle rise and fall of my breasts
Butterfly wings will carry my laughter with each pulse

Tiny blooming buds radiating my smile
Upon hearing your voice
As everything returns to life,
So too shall you, in everything you see

I am all around you
I always have been
And will always be
Like you are always
In all that I see.

Churning, Turning, Swirling

My heart shredded
Like confetti
Strewn about
Invisibly

A glimpse of daylight
Then back underground
Churning slowly forward
And making no sound

My lungs gasp
Searching for air
Choking back
Without care

And I'm still churning
Stepping, moving, as I can
Reaching for the lantern
Struggling to plan

My head swirling
Like a whirlpool
In the mirror
I see a fool?

Churning onward still
Even when I stop
To rest and retreat
Before the expected 'pop!'

My body cooling
No more open doors
A key was words
And I was yours

Slow wheels turning
Slipping backward into fear
Screeching brakes
Is now the sound I hear

Love no more
Weeping still
You won't close the door
Yet ...

I must keep wheels turning
Forward, onward, through
Beyond the darkness that's held me
To the light of something new.

What is Love?

In the distant glow of a
Sunset cascading over an icy peak
As two hands interlace
Woven as one.

Amid the fabled stories and
The real tears shed
After loss or betrayal
Have created their invisible scars.

Within the sigh of relief of a hundred
Nights of longing
To touch, hold, see, someone
Again, for the first time.

Give Way!

The velvet darkness of night
Closes in softly

To touch it is warm
With a cavernous depth

Still empty and longing
Holding promise

Chocolate air like satin
Envelops me
Underneath there lies a question
The question
The question without answer, answered every day.

Worn like a mantel, doubt
Shrouds the light
Worn like a shield, doubt
Conceals

Give way. Give way!
Love is the only shield.
Love is the shroud.

27 November 2012

Unified Duality

I am everything and nothing all at once.
The barren land, the fruitful sea.
Look into my eyes where there is beauty and stillness,
The chaos of the world is quiet.

Weak, I am surrounded by strength.
Strong, I feel weakness grab hold of me.

There is no divergence that is
Not already parted and divine.
No union that is not joined
And divided at once.

Everything apart, and nothing together
Like fruit trees laden with bounty
Dispersed on the ground

Everything together and nothing apart
The universe in an atom and the ocean in a tear.

I know love.
Love is the harp on which I play peace.
I know fear.
Sadness drums like tribes calling to war.

I know.
I know and I am.

Never ceasing.
Blinking only to see again.

Never ending.
Embracing and running away together, alone.

Everything and nothing.
All at once.

Breath and dying in arid waters.
Searching, seeing – never finding.

Everything and nothing.
All.
At once.

I know I am.

Branded Speechless

How can I tell you
In the short time
Brimming with emotion
I was silenced

The love, the passion, we had
Without words
Your skin, eyes, voice,
Burning my heart

Flying like a bird
Free to experiment and feel
Like never before
Life

Living in you
Thinking of you, in our distance
I have fear, peace.
What can we ever be?

My love, my friend
You have touched my soul
Like a tiger, a harlequin
An angel

You have branded me
On my heart
How can I tell you?
I can't.

circa 1990

Through the Cracks…Love

Roaring above the chatterboxes
And truth
Silently stealing
From our warehouses
Of joy

There exists a quiet desperation
That craves to be
Heard
Seen
Counted

To exist beyond what's known.

A broken heart opens to
Release its pain
Hidden
Tucked away and concealed
For all to see.

Through the cracks I can still see beauty,
Through the tears, joy.
The gift of my heart is its sight.
With lifetimes lived in each blink.

Stolen glances across the room
I know what others would say,
"To be lovers it's much too soon."
Yet I can't tear myself away.

Captivated
I need your embrace.
Your smile,
Removes all time or place.

I will keep you with me
Here
Now
Always
Until we are no more.

The truth is
Lovers never lose.

ABOUT THE AUTHOR

Martina E. Faulkner has been called a Mystic for the modern age: part visionary and philosopher, part writer and teacher, and part healer and guide. Always writing, Martina has been sharing her inspirational prose for over a decade, while quietly writing poetry for herself, until now.

This is Martina's first book of collected poems, delving into the very human experiences of love, loss, and hope. The theme of hope is prevalent throughout all of Martina's work and teachings. As an author, Martina uses words to teach, share, and express what it means to be both human and divine – what it means to have hope.

From this perspective, Martina combines her experience and expertise (as a Certified Life Coach, Therapist, Reiki Master Teacher, and gifted Psychic/Intuitive) in new and innovative ways that serve to inspire others to create more meaningful and joy-filled lives.

Martina currently resides in the Chicago area with her family and her dog. She enjoys being in nature or pursuing her other creative interests, such as photography, painting, and jewelry-making.

www.martinafaulkner.com

www.inspirebytes.com

www.ingramcontent.com/pod-product-compliance
Lightning Source LLC
Chambersburg PA
CBHW031504040426
42444CB00007B/1205